About the TLS

The *Times Literary Supplement* was born in January 1902. Its first ever front page bashfully stated that 'during the Parliamentary session Literary Supplements to "The Times" will appear as often as may be necessary in order to keep abreast with the more important publications of the day'. Fortunately, the question of necessity was not left in the hands of literary journalists (who, we can imagine, might occasionally push for a holiday or two), and the title became a weekly one. A few years later, the *TLS* split entirely from *The Times*.

Since then, we have prided ourselves on being the world's leading magazine for culture and ideas. Our guiding principle for the selection of pieces remains the same as it ever has been: is it interesting; and is it beautifully written? Over the years, our contributors have included the very best writers and thinkers in the world: from

Virginia Woolf to Seamus Heaney, Sylvia Plath to Susan Sontag, Milan Kundera to Christopher Hitchens, Patricia Highsmith to Martin Scorsese.

The book you are holding is part of a brand-new imprint, *TLS Books*, by which we are striving to bring more beautiful writing to a wider public. We hope you enjoy it. If you want to read more from us, you'll find a special trial subscription offer to the *TLS* at the back of this book.

In an ever-quickening culture of flipness and facility, fake news and Facebook, the *TLS* is determined to be part of the counter-culture of quality. We believe in expertise, breadth and depth. We believe in the importance of ideas, and the transformative power of art. And we believe that, in reading the *TLS* – in whatever form, be it in a magazine, online or in a book – you are supporting a set of values that we have been proud to uphold for more than a hundred years. So thank you for that.

Stig Abell, 11th Editor of the *TLS*
London, 2019

The
Hero

Also by Lee Child

A Wanted Man (2012)
Never Go Back (2013)
Personal (2014)
Make Me (2015)
Night School (2016)
The Midnight Line (2017)
Past Tense (2018)
Blue Moon (2019)

NON-FICTION
Jack Reacher's Rules (2012)

The
Hero

Lee Child

TLS

TLS Books
An imprint of HarperCollins*Publishers*
1 London Bridge Street
London SE1 9GF

The-TLS.co.uk

First published in Great Britain in 2019 by TLS Books

1

Illustrations copyright © Ella Baron 2019

A catalogue record for this book is
available from the British Library

ISBN 978-0-00-835578-4

Typeset in Publico Text
Printed and bound in Great Britain by
CPI Group (UK) Ltd, Croydon

The Hero

L et's start with opium. That venerable poppy grew wild and natural after the retreat of the last Ice Age, across a broad band of territory stretching from Asia Minor to the Mediterranean to North Africa. We know from the archaeological record that New Stone Age farmers were interested in it. A carefully curated stash of seeds, about seven thousand years old, was discovered near the Mediterranean Sea; seventeen other New Stone Age sites throughout what we now call Europe show evidence of opium use five or six thousand years ago; and the first deliberate cultivation of the poppy, as opposed to its casual collection, seems to have happened in Mesopotamia over five thousand years ago, organized by the local Sumerians, who called their crop *hul gil*, which translates as 'the joy plant'.

I would love to know who tried it first. I would love to know who tried anything first. Who first dug up a strange root or random tuber and thought, hey, you know what – maybe I should cook this and eat it? In particular, I would love to know how many died trying. Our species seems to be restless and curious to a degree that seems almost unhinged. Recent research concerning the Neanderthal people shows them to have been pretty much the opposite of what we have long assumed – they were intelligent, bigger-brained, better animals than us, stronger, faster, healthier, more durable, better toolmakers, caring, compassionate, gentle, artistic and organized. But they seem to have been constitutionally timid. Their settlements migrated slowly, cautiously and sensibly. Often a new settlement would be within sight of a previous settlement. In particular travel over water seems never to have been attempted, unless the far shore was clearly visible. By contrast, our own ancestors, *Homo sapiens*, went anywhere and everywhere, many of them, we assume, to their doom. Not cautious or sensible at all. The consensus – in what I suppose we could call psychological archaeology – seems to be that *Homo neanderthalensis* was painfully rational, and *Homo sapiens* was batshit crazy.

Crazy enough, certainly, for one of them to notice the pretty red flower, to scratch its immature seed pod, to watch the sticky latex ooze out, and then to think, hey, you know what – maybe I should collect this stuff and dry it, and then suck it or chew it or smoke it. I would like to meet that person. Certainly his or her inspiration was way more complicated than, for instance, finding a carrot and deciding to try a bite. Restless and curious indeed. (Although smoking is a misnomer – the latex was not itself set on fire, but indirectly heated, and the active ingredients were inhaled as they gassed off. Vaping, five thousand years ago. Nothing new under the sun.) The effect, then as now, was of a deeply warm, hugely satisfying contentment, washing unstoppably over the user, leaving him or her laid out and passive for hours at a time, inert and endlessly contemplative. As a result, the opium poppy's scientific name is *Papaver somniferum*, which is Latin for 'the poppy that carries you to sleep'.

Of course the problem with an extract from a plant growing wild and natural – or even farmed, given good years and bad – was that dosage was fundamentally unpredictable. The sixteenth-century physician Gabriel Fallopius complained bitterly that opium tended to be either too weak or too strong, and if weak it didn't help, and if strong it was exceedingly dangerous. An overdose caused the victim's breathing to slow down, and down, and down, until it stopped altogether. Not good. So began a quest to isolate the active ingredients, in order to deliver them in known and reliable doses.

Like most things to do with practical chemistry, not much happened until the nineteenth century, when, between 1804 and 1817, a

German pharmacist named Friedrich Sertürner zeroed-in on a particular compound that made up about twelve per cent of the latex by weight. It seemed to be where the action was. The other eighty-eight per cent was window dressing. Sertürner got better at getting the good stuff out, but showed less finesse in his experimental methodology; his indiscriminate test doses nearly killed him and the three young boys he recruited to help. Restless and curious and almost unhinged. But in the end he lived to announce he had successfully isolated the compound, which would henceforth reliably deliver the wave of hugely satisfying contentment, and had the happy side effect of also being the most effective painkiller so far known in human history. Sertürner named his newly naked chemical after the Greek god of dreams. He called it *morphine*.

Morphine did well in the subsequent decades, especially after the invention of the hypodermic syringe as a delivery system. The American Civil War became a gigantic testing ground for its painkilling abilities. It was great. Wounded soldiers called it 'God's Own Medicine'. But it was extremely addictive. Opium itself had long been known to be addictive – a sixteenth-century Venetian visitor observing far-gone Turkish users reported that without their fix they 'quickly die'. And that was with the eighty-eight per cent window dressing included. Morphine was the real thing, all the time. In America the 1860s ended with millions of addicts. The same was true elsewhere, albeit less spectacular in terms of numbers. So began a new quest, to deliver the wave of contentment, and the painkilling, but without the addiction.

In true British style, the (then presumed) solution was hit upon in 1874 – perhaps by accident – by an English chemist named C. R. Alder Wright, who then quickly abandoned the project, perhaps as uninteresting. The same discovery was then made again, more than twenty years later, and independently, and perhaps also accidentally, by a German chemist named Felix Hoffmann. Hoffmann was trying to synthesize codeine, which is morphine's baby brother, a chemically similar, but less potent and less addictive substance. Instead his new discovery turned out to be twice as strong as morphine, twice as good at delivering the wave of contentment, and above all not in the least little bit addictive. Or so Hoffmann claimed at the time.

His product swept the world, delivering every bit of the longed-for feeling, deeply warm, hugely satisfying, unstoppable. Twice as fit for purpose as morphine, and way better than opium. It was put in cough syrup for children, and tinctures for anxious women. But the non-addictive part of the deal was a lie. Hoffmann's product was in fact horrifically addictive. Lives were ruined, people died, crime was rampant. (But corporate fortunes were made.)

What did Hoffmann name his product, that at best left its users laid out and passive for hours at a time, inert and endlessly contemplative,

and at worst ruined their lives and killed them?
He called it *heroin*, from the German for *heroic*.
Why that word?

The best linguist I know is my daughter Ruth. Her main enthusiasm is the deep structure of language, but she runs a lively sideline in English etymology, fascinated by the origins of words, their drifting meanings and the way in which their choice and usage subtly influence the mood and temper of the clauses in which they appear. Once we were driven from New York to Philadelphia – me for a book event at the Free Library, she hitching a ride to visit old college friends – and we talked the whole two hours about the use of a gerund on an advertising billboard we saw. Did the gerund somehow offer openness, warmth, inclusion, invitation? Mostly she talked, and I listened. Very rarely do I know something she doesn't. My only score in recent years was the origin of the English word 'rival' – but I had an unfair advantage: I have a law degree, and studied the history of English common law, and knew that the long-ago ground-zero issue for all kinds of torts and liabilities was bodies of water, in terms of upstream depletion and downstream flooding and so on. Hence rival, from the Latin *rivalis*, one who competes over a river.

But for all her personal rules and grammar-based rigour about structure, Ruth is very permissive in terms of the prescriptive-descriptive linguistic debate. She's happy for words to change their meanings. Grammatical conventions, too. She feels language is what its users need it to be. She won't exclude people for a lack of facility or fluency. Not like the ancient Greeks, who had utter contempt for those who couldn't speak their language. 'Barbarian' is a Greek word, meaning a savage – not necessarily a violent, rampaging or physical savage, but one whose savagery consisted solely in not being able to speak Greek. To the Greeks, all that such people could manage was baa-baa-baa, like sheep. Hence ba-ba-rian. Ruth is not like that.

I'm somewhere between the two poles. I think words must have commonly agreed meanings, otherwise all we can ever say to each other is baa-baa-baa. If someone arranges to meet me at the baseball stadium, I'll show up there, not the ice hockey arena. If someone asks for a cigarette, I'll give them one, not a pen or a key or a handkerchief. And so on, and so forth. Words should be more like knives than pillows. Which is not to say they should never change. I'm perfectly happy with the migration of a word like rival. No doubt its modern meaning was first introduced as a metaphor. Or more likely, the very first time out, as a simile: *You two are competing like ... like ... rivals!* It's a good simile and therefore a good subsequent migration, preserving as it does the core emotional truth of the original, before transferring it to a new context.

I'm also happy with adoptions, like, say, *addict* (since we've mentioned many millions of them) – from the Latin *addictus*, which meant a debtor awarded as a slave to his creditor. That kind of thing didn't happen any more, but when a new word was needed (not long after Sertürner first isolated morphine, unsurprisingly), *addict* was an astute choice, with the shame of indebtedness suggesting the shame of submission to a dependency, both blended with the strong, almost literal, slavery metaphor. I'm content that over many centuries 'nice' moved from disapproval to approbation, and that over the same span 'bully' moved in the other direction. I can deal with stuff invented five minutes ago. When I was a kid, 'sick' was what you pretended to be to get a day off work. Now it's the best thing ever. Soon it won't be. Soon it will be forgotten, like the groovy words we used, back in the day. All good.

Except that, it must be said, occasionally common sense yields to pedantry. My personal irritant is 'dilapidated'. Right there in the middle of the word is the Latin *lapis*, which means *stone*. A dilapidated building is one from which stones have been removed or taken out, possibly stolen, possibly to be reused or repurposed. Hence a wooden hut cannot be dilapidated. A brick house cannot be dilapidated. They were never lapidated to start with. Hence frequent irritation. Such are the perils of a classical education. Education is different now, but it wasn't all that different before my time, not for a couple of centuries. Any well-educated person anywhere in Europe would have had a solid grounding in the classics. Certainly the coiner of *addict* did. Is it an exaggeration to say that Latin and Greek were known quantities in households with more books than a lone family bible? Probably, but if a member of such a household completed any kind of undergraduate or postgraduate work, there would have been significant accumulated exposure to the classical languages, and the cultures they represented, and their stories, their myths and their legends. Obviously old Gabriel Fallopius knew all that stuff. Certainly Friedrich Sertürner knew all about the Greek god of dreams. (And was probably ready to argue for forty-five minutes why it was indeed *dreams*, not *sleep*.) In the eighteenth and nineteenth centuries, anyone educated in Germany as a pharmacist would have known that kind of thing.

Which meant Felix Hoffmann did, too. So why did he call it heroin?

E ven before I learned it was so, I always vaguely assumed 'hero' was ancient Greek. It just sounded right. I further vaguely assumed even in modern times the word might signify something complicated, central and still marginally relevant in today's Greek heritage. Naively I assumed I was proved right, the first time I came to New York, in 1974. I ate in Greek diners with grand and legacy-heavy names like Parthenon and Acropolis, and from Greek corner delis, some of which had no name at all, but every single establishment had 'hero sandwiches' on the menu. This was partly simple respect for tradition, I thought, like the blue-and-white take-away coffee cups, and also perhaps a cultural imperative, a ritual genuflection, but probably most of all marketing, as if to say, *eat this mighty meal and you too could be a legend celebrated for millennia.* Like Wheaties, the breakfast of champions.

But no. 'Hero' was a simple phonetic spelling in English of the Greek word 'gyro'. It was how New Yorkers said it. A hero sandwich was a gyro sandwich, filled with street-meat thinly carved from a large wad that rotated slowly against a source of heat. Like the kebab shops we got in Britain a few years later. Central to modern culture, perhaps, but not to ancient heritage.

Even so, 'hero' remains an ancient Greek word, and like 'barbarian', the concept behind it must have been shaped by – indeed, subliminally specified in great detail by – that ancient culture's needs, concerns, desires, prejudices, aspirations and fears. All stories have a purpose, and the older and more durable the story, the more elemental the purpose is likely to be. Figuring out the purpose can be difficult. Fiction was a strange invention. To fit it into evolution's merciless logic is challenging.

These days we know an amazing amount about human origins. While I was studying law, my then girlfriend Jane (later and still my wife) was studying prehistory and archaeology. I'm not sure there's ever a fun time to study law, but that particular period was terrific for her subject. 'Lucy' was about to be discovered – the fossilized remains of a female of the hominin species *Australopithecus afarensis*, more than three million years old. She was an upright bipedal walker. She was a fully mature adult, at the age of twelve. She may have been killed by falling out of a tree. Somehow she captured people's imaginations. Not at all like us, yet somehow she was, way back in the primeval past.

It turned out she was only about halfway back. The forty-plus years since we graduated have seen an ongoing tsunami of discovery and analysis. I remain fascinated, and I keep up with the news as well as I can. The last common ancestor we had with anything else was about seven million years ago. Since then we have been evolving on our own, one hard-won generation after another. The length of a generation was at first short and animal-like, but they grew slowly to the present-day when a generation is taken to last twenty-five years or so. The arithmetic is therefore a moving target and hard to pin down, but a fair guess might be that we have been evolving on our own for perhaps 400,000 generations so far. I could picture my mother, with my grandmother standing behind her, not very different, and her mother behind her, again not very different, and behind her an endless line of 399,997 other women, each very similar to the one in front and the one behind, but cumulatively receding toward a small, apelike appearance. Lucy would be about number 200,000 down the line (if she's in our ancestral lineage; some think she isn't). Collectively and personally that line represents unlikely and astonishing reproductive success – every one of those 400,000 women survived long enough to have a female child, who survived long enough to have a female child of her own, and so on, through Ice Ages and million-year heatwaves and famines and epidemics, until it got to my mother. At that point the unbroken seven-million-year matriarchal line came to an abrupt end, because although my mother survived long enough to have four children, they were all boys. No big deal. Happens all the time. But nevertheless a sad end. After 400,000 successful passes of the baton, there is no new woman to stand in front of my mother.

Those seven million years were mostly hard going. There was no triumphant and irresistible march toward where we are today. Most of the time we were close to the bottom of the pile. The best place to find early bones is a hyena's den. We got dragged there, after the alpha predators were done with us. We were weak, slow, often wounded, often hungry. Going nowhere, basically. Then something happened.

The whole basis of evolution is random mutation. Each one of those 400,000 women was similar to the woman in front and the woman behind, but they weren't identical. Most mutations are small, so-what, no-real-difference things. They come and go. Some mutations are debilitating. They die out fast. Some are beneficial, and go on to spread widely, because of enhanced genetic success over possibly hundreds of generations. Some are super-beneficial, and therefore spread even faster. Which is what seems to have happened with our brains. Suddenly they got bigger. I would love to have been a fly on the wall during the early stages of this development. Some folks must have been making out like bandits. Their genetic success was so overwhelming that in what looks from a distance like a mere blip of time, the fossil record shows our brains became suddenly and impressively huge.

There's a chicken-and-egg argument about whether our new brain capacity then allowed for expanded cerebral activities, or whether expanding cerebral activities themselves drove the increase in our brain capacity. Or both. Either way, one of the new cerebral activities was crucial. It turned us from weak, middle-of-the-pack prey into the most powerful animal on earth. That activity was language.

Not simple language. We almost certainly already had that. Many animals do. Prairie dogs have different sounds for airborne predators and ground-based predators. What we got was syntactical language. The huge increase in bandwidth gave us the ability to speculate, strategize, coordinate, discuss, predict and develop a plan B ahead of time. Whereas eleven humans had previously been a mid-table team, now suddenly they were one giant animal, lethal and effective. Suddenly in a manner of speaking, of course. Even rapid evolutionary change must feel slow at the time.

This all happened about 10,000 women ago. The previous 390,000 had not been able to speculate, strategize, coordinate, discuss, predict, or develop a plan B ahead of time. Now things were different. The advantages were obvious. One of the books kicking around our undergraduate bedroom was *Stone Age*

Economics by Marshall Sahlins. In it he made the startling argument that no one will ever again be as affluent as Stone Age humans during the best of Stone Age times. For millennia they had everything they needed all around them, in great abundance, and they became very good at getting it. Sophisticated language was their secret weapon.

Now, quite rightly, scientists stick to just the facts, ma'am, and what they can prove, and so on. Some argue about hyoid bones, and how upright bipedal posture displaced our larynxes and certain other tissues, all in a downward direction, which came in useful later, because they were found to be newly capable of the variety and subtlety of sounds required by a complex spoken language. That is what a scientist reports. A novelist wants to imagine what those people were saying. Is such speculation legitimate? I don't really care. Such musings are merely a personal enthusiasm. I'm not trying to convince anyone of anything. I'm not entering evidence into the academic record.

And anyway, sometimes such speculation works really well. Another of the books kicking around our undergraduate bedroom was *The Descent of Woman* by Elaine Morgan. Morgan was a Welsh screenwriter. Among much else she wrote episodes for *Doctor Finlay's Casebook*. She won two BAFTAs, two Writers' Guild awards, a Prix Italia, and the Royal Television Society's Writer of the Year award for her serialization of Vera Brittain's *Testament of Youth*. She also had a keen amateur interest in evolutionary anthropology and human origins. She was irritated by the contemporary male-centred pop science approach taken by Desmond Morris, among others. She saw it as a classic example of history as 'his story'. For example, Morris theorized that male humans lost their body hair so that they could sweat better, as they charged around the savannah like the mighty hunters they were. OK, Morgan thought, but why did women lose even more of their body hair, while doing nothing but sitting around at home, on bottoms Morris claimed were made ample for that very purpose?

Morgan took what we knew, and applied a writer's focused imagination to figure out how we got from there to here. Why are humans the only mammals with vestigially webbed fingers? Why are humans the only mammals who cry salt tears? Why does what remains of our body hair flow with water? And so on. Morgan's conclusion was that a significant number of our ancestors had spent a long period – certainly hundreds of thousands of years – living on the seashore, half in and half out of the water, either driven out of the forests and away from the savannahs by competition for resources, or forced to seek refuge from rising temperatures. Hers was a major contribution to what is known as the *aquatic ape hypothesis*. Naturally she was derided for being an amateur, and worse, a woman. But now nearly fifty years later there is some acceptance of the theory. The kind of nutrients in shellfish and seafood are excellent for brain development. Body language and gesture were useless while bobbing around in the shallows, which might have spurred vocal communication. Some ancient hominid fossils show growths in and deformities of the ear, identical to those found in present-day divers and surfers. Human babies are born coated in *vernix caseosa*, a waxy, waterproof short-term protectant for their newborn skin, as are harbour seals and some sea lions. And so on. Like I said, sometimes speculation works really well.

So what were they saying, ten thousand generations ago? Remember, these people were not yet modern. Paleoanthropologists guess that humans were cognitively, behaviourally and physically modern only about 1,750 women ago. In other words, if you had a time machine and could go get an orphan baby from that period and bring her home, she would grow up exactly like every other modern kid, with an iPad and an iPhone and texting and petty high school dramas. Before that period, it wouldn't work. The kid would seem odd. Ten thousand generations was a very long way before that period. Humans were still very primitive, albeit using language. But using it, I imagine, in a strictly functional and transactional manner. Stone Age affluence was about a technical balance between supply and demand, during the best of times. It didn't imply a permanent cushy lifestyle with plenty of leisure. For most of the Stone Age, every day was filled with work and danger and difficulty. Hunting big game was exhausting and perilous. Foraging required extensive coordination to be efficient. Meanwhile other predators were enjoying their own take on supply and demand. An unsettling percentage of human remains from the Old Stone Age have bite marks on them. Perhaps night-time fires had to be kept burning, and a guard organized.

In other words, I imagine they were talking non-fiction. I think at first it was inevitable. The entire species-saving power of complex communication was predicated upon everyone telling the truth. Or, more technically, upon people not yet realizing language could be used any other way. If someone said the woolly mammoths were in the next valley over, but knew they weren't really, then although the statement itself might have been dazzling in its fluency and its variety and its subtlety, it would have caused the whole evolutionary value of language to be immediately and fatally short-circuited, because then language would have been of absolutely no practical help to the situation, and therefore it would very quickly have become just another small, so-what, no-real-difference curiosity. But it didn't, because my 9,998-times great grandmother took it seriously.

At this point, because I'm an amateur and a man, someone will point out that my belief in early truthful non-fiction is naive. Even chimpanzees tell lies, they will say. Which is true. Bad chimps have been observed chattering the phrase for *Get out! Get out! There's a predator coming!* when really there wasn't, so that the good chimp would drop his banana in a panic, so that the bad chimp could grab it up and eat it. To which I say yes, I'm sure we did that too, way, way, way back, as some kind of ancient animal reflex, someplace very early among the first 390,000 women, when we were still on a par with chimpanzees, cognitively. But not 10,000 women ago. They were too smart. What other definitive evolutionary gain has ever been given away by internal sabotage?

The Old Stone Age was very long. As its name suggests, it started with the first use of stone tools, which was about 200,000 women ago, around the time Lucy was falling out of a tree. As can be imagined, with evolving and developing participants, progress started slow, stayed slow for a long time, and then got exponentially faster and faster, with a marked and sophisticated acceleration about 10,000 women ago (when language started, unsurprisingly). A new toolmaking method was developed – the prepared-core technique, which had faint pre-echoes of modern mass production. Previously flint knappers had made, say, a hand axe out of whatever lump of stone lay closest by. Now the lumps of stone were carefully pre-sorted, by shape, size and grain, so that finishing an article might require perhaps only minimal further work. Productivity exploded. Tiny stone tools called *microliths* were invented, and used to make the first composite weapons, as arrowheads or spear tips.

Probably very little of this progression was learned from contact with other bands or tribes. At that time the human population was still tiny, and it was under constant intense pressure from the climate. A period of extremely harsh cold began about 2,000 women ago (perhaps my 1,998-times great grandmother is wearing a heavy animal fur, as she waits patiently in line) and about eight hundred women later, the individual standing 1,198 places behind my grandma was one of perhaps only two thousand living women in the whole of what we now call Europe. Only the very strongest survived that vicious population bottleneck, and the very best at speculating, strategizing, coordinating, discussing, predicting and developing a plan B ahead of time. Probably a plan C and a plan D too, under the circumstances. Truthful non-fiction carried the day.

But it was increasingly mixed in with something new and strange. At some point those women started talking about things that hadn't happened to people who didn't exist. This was not lying, in a sense that threatened the evolutionary value of language. This was a radical mental jump in a completely different direction, never before attempted. This was imagining a parallel or theoretical universe, where things could happen, based on experience, but not constrained by fact. In other words, they invented fiction. We don't know when exactly. A spoken word is not a discoverable artefact. It is gone forever, as soon as the last echo dies away to silence. But perhaps we can calibrate it against other early arts. We know the woman 2,998 places behind my grandma was already playing music. Bone flutes have been discovered, with holes drilled for fingering. We know the woman 500 places ahead of the flautist was already painting. We have seen her eerie work in many different locations. Both music and painting require technological innovation – flutes and drums, pigments and brushes – whereas storytelling requires none. We already had our voices, well capable of various and subtle expressions. So probably storytelling came before music or art, possibly by a large margin. Perhaps the woman 4,998 places behind my grandma was the first to talk about things that hadn't happened to people who didn't exist. But why would she?

She was still living deep in prehistory. The Darwinian rules still applied. No behaviour could endure unless it made it at least slightly more likely the participant would still be alive in the morning. There was no room for frivolity. The best of times were gone. The golden days were over. The weather was starting to change, megafauna populations were declining, other predators were getting increasingly desperate. How could fiction help? Which it had to, definitively, or it would have fizzled out into a small, so-what, no-real-difference byway. Which we know didn't happen. Fiction became curiously central to our natures. Our official name is *Homo sapiens sapiens*, but some say it should be *pan narrans*, the storytelling ape. Stories must have had the capacity to help us significantly, or why would they have appeared just as hunger and danger returned? First the big brains, then complex language, then millennia of reality-based planning, and now fictions, just as the ice sheets crept south and the bottleneck rushed toward us. Inspired use of all four of those factors got the few survivors through.

Stories not least among them. Encouraging, empowering, emboldening stories, that somehow made it more likely the listener would still be alive in the morning. Perhaps the first was about a girl who left the cave and met a sabretoothed tiger. But she turned and ran and made it home safe! In other words, a kind of parable, reassuring and educational, about how disaster can be faced and survived. You can find yourself on the edge of the cliff, but you don't have to fall off. Encouraging, empowering, emboldening. Perhaps a hundred mothers later, the story grew. A girl left the cave and met a sabre-toothed tiger, but she had her axe with her and she killed the tiger with a single blow! She came home triumphant! That's the birth of the thriller right there, 4,900 women ago.

At this point it's worth asking what the Neanderthals were doing at the time. Did they have complex language? Almost certainly. Their brains were bigger than ours. It's hard to reverse-engineer the evident success of their settlements without assuming the benefits of sophisticated communication. So they too marched toward the bottleneck, like we did, with brains and language and reality-based planning. But did they have fiction on top? Or were they too painfully rational to countenance talking about things that hadn't happened to people who didn't exist? Was that radical jump in their heads just not available? Was the wiring missing? We will never know, of course, but it's worth noting the Neanderthals went extinct, not long after the icy cold bit down hard. Our own population was in free fall, but theirs went faster. Then it died out completely. The final end of their line is barely visible in the far, far distance, about level with the woman standing 1,800 places behind my grandma.

Maybe three factors weren't enough. Maybe fiction was the essential fourth. All we know for sure is in the whole of Europe maybe two thousand men and two thousand women staggered out the other side of the bottleneck, all of them batshit crazy, all of them armed, as we know from what we inherited from them, with a ferocious will to live, and a deep love of story.

Europe's human population recovered over the course of many generations, until the woman standing, say, 500 places behind my grandma found herself living in a relatively stable situation. The details of her life had changed a little, compared to the women earlier in line. There was less hunting of large animals, and more of small animals, exploiting further advances in very small stone tools and weapons. There was wider-spread and more variegated gathering of produce. Probably she lived on the coast or a riverbank, where the food supply was richest and most various. She didn't know it, and she certainly wouldn't have cared, but by then she was living in what future archaeologists would call the Mesolithic – the Middle Stone Age, from the

Greek *mesos*, middle, and *lithos*, stone – which was a short ten-thousand-year interval before things changed again. It was a simple, straightforward, satisfactory lifestyle.

Her location was her only real problem. Way north of where she was, out of sight and out of mind (and certainly beyond Mesolithic comprehension) the mile-thick ice sheets were still melting, and sea levels were rising. Perhaps she lived in a fertile valley bottom near a rushing river, with plenty of fish, and game in the copses, and ruminants wandering the wild pastures, and roots and berries galore. All good. Except now that's the bottom of the North Sea. Possibly her fifty-times great granddaughter was the first to notice. She had to move up the hill a little. And then again. As it happens she went west. As did her daughter, and her granddaughter, and her great granddaughter, and so on, until eventually the woman 400 places behind my grandma arrived on a landmass we would recognize as shaped like modern Britain. She brought everything with her, everything she had inherited from the two thousand breeding pairs who had survived the glaciation, plus everything the subsequent four hundred generations had learned and passed on. She brought brains, language, reality-based planning, a ferocious will to live, and a deep love of story.

S tories need characters. At first I suppose they were generic and symbolic. The girl who left the village, the boy who outran a bear, the old man who would surely come along, any day now, to tell them where the aurochs were. I suppose some stories proved more popular than others, and more successful in meeting their emboldening aims. Probably last-gasp narrow escapes worked well. And sudden last-minute rescues, when all seemed lost. The characters in those popular stories would soon become eponymous. The girl who, the boy who, the man who, the woman who. Not the supporting characters, if there were any. Not the boy who got it wrong, or the girl who got eaten. From this early point onward, I think we focused on main characters. At first as types, probably.

Stories became synonymous with the type of main character in them: The brave girl, the artful dodger, the wise old woman.

Of course, it's important to remember that none of those people actually existed. They were all made up. There are only two real people in fiction – the storyteller and the listener. The story proceeds based on the teller's aims and the listener's needs. If the listener needs light entertainment, and the teller aims to be loved, then light entertainment is what the listener will get. But if the listener needs reassurance of some kind, or consolation, and the teller aims to better equip her family for future trials, then the story will likely be suspenseful in nature, replete with dangers and perils, over which a memorable character will eventually triumph in a decisive manner, such that the listener finishes the tale with a tight and determined smile, with moist eyes fixed on the distant horizon.

In order to keep memorable characters inspiring, they grew steadily, in both complexity and powers. Sooner or later they got a name, and a backstory and parentage, and possibly a lineage that linked back to people in earlier stories. And sooner or later they also got size and strength, and tremendous endurance, and nobility of purpose. They became larger than life, the better to stand out and lead. If they got too much larger than life, they were given supernatural explanations.

Bottom line, they became idealized examples of desired behaviours. But idealized by who? Desired by who? Remember, all characters in fiction are invented by the storyteller, to fit the storyteller's agenda, which might be subconscious or subliminal, or might be absolutely in the front of her mind.

Who were the storytellers? We know very little about social organization during the Old and Middle Stone Ages. There may have been very little. The hunter-gatherer lifestyle is essentially cooperative and egalitarian. There was probably an overriding loyalty to the band or the group, but within it, maybe informality

ruled. In which case the flautists and the paint-
ers and the storytellers would rise and fall on
merit alone. For storytellers, the merit would
come in two parts. First the composition of a
compelling narrative, sometimes extemporane-
ously. (Although these days the best 'spontane-
ous' performances are rehearsed within an inch
of their lives, and I don't see why it would have
been any different in the Middle Stone Age.)
The second part was a talent for performance.
Maybe even for acting the story out, with
drama, and expression and timing. Now 'voice'
is taken to be a vague stylistic issue to do with
writing. Then it was literally a human voice,
warm, spellbinding, seductive, drawing people
in. The *New York Times* bestseller of the day was
the storyteller with twenty rapt listeners at her
feet. Not like the guy in the next hut along, with
five fidgeters. Obviously that guy is not going to
make it. Obscurity beckons for him. His audience of five will join her twenty. She'll become
a minor star, like the guy who finds truffles, or
the woman whose dog catches deer.

Then something very strange happened. Weirder than language, weirder than fiction. In fact almost inexplicable, and completely irrational. Unhinged in a bad way. The Neanderthals would never have done it. The woman standing 248 places behind my grandma started farming. Which produced a whole mess of issues. Ownership of land had to be invented as a concept. Nomadic lifestyles were abandoned. We ate what we grew, which was sometimes a lot, and sometimes not much at all.

It was very bad for us. Before-and-after archaeological studies show farming made us smaller, weaker and sicker. One of the books kicking around our forty-plus-years-married bedroom is *Against the Grain*, by James C. Scott. In it he challenges the easy and unthinking assumption – to which I plead retrospectively guilty – that farming was somehow progress, natural and inevitable. Scott says it wasn't. He wants to know why we would abandon a relatively pleasant lifestyle – finding truffles, catching deer, having time for stories – in favour of drudgery, disease and malnutrition. His final conclusion technically exonerates the woman 248 places behind my grandma. It turns out she didn't start farming. At least not voluntarily. Her mistake was not to resist harder, when she was forced to start farming.

Scott's analysis was that the five hundred post-glacial generations of Mesolithic hunter-gatherers had indeed lived a stable, simple, straightforward, satisfactory life, marked by notable levels of cooperation and informal equality. But that also, all along, the human brain had harboured notions of hierarchy and elitism. Some people wanted power and control. It was a long time coming. But eventually, for an unlikely combination of reasons, the time was right. People were sold the idea they should become subsistence farmers, in service to unpredictable crops and weather, in virtual slavery, and sometimes literal slavery. Reluctant adopters were coerced. Wheat was favoured by the elite as a crop, because it was energy- and value-dense, and easily bagged-up, and therefore easily taxed. One bag for you, one bag for me. Or whatever the rate was. (Did the bigwigs then go chill out and smoke dope? Archaeology says someone started to, right there, right then.) There would be excise raids, and penalties for low weight or late payment. The whole proposition must have been a hard sell. Recent research from the Mediterranean rim suggests that increasing population density might have been a factor. Encounters with other roving tribes might have become much more common, and possibly not pleasant – possibly even rivalrous. The idea was sold that people needed to band together, in one secure place, even at the expense of their own individual best interests, in order to resist the external enemy. Which if true was the birth of fascism, right there, 5,000 years ago. (From the Latin *fascis*, a bundle of separate sticks, tightly strapped together.)

Story must have played a part in that hard sell. The entire purpose of story is to manipulate. Previously who was doing the manipulating didn't matter very much. It was always just some random person, with talent and energy, and no real agenda beyond some kind of empowering encouragement, which was intended to help the community as a whole anyway. But now there was a state, however rudimentary, and a government. There was an elite, and a hierarchy stretching out below them. There was power and control. The New Stone Age. A new system. Perhaps too long ago and too small and too prototype-crude to be given names from later periods, but all authoritarian and totalitarian governments need to control the story. From this point on, who was doing the manipulating mattered a lot. From this point on, there was an establishment, with powers of approval and prohibition that swung from the vague to the admonitory to the savage. From this point on, to get ahead of ourselves for a moment, there were official heroes, and there were folk heroes.

The stories told around the time the woman 138 places behind my grandma was alive are the first we know in any detail. They are the great Greek legends, most notably Homer's *Iliad* and *Odyssey*, respectively the oldest and second-oldest extant works of Western literature. To Homer (whoever he was, or however many different people he was) a 'hero' was a warrior who lived and died in pursuit of honour, and – specifically – had fought in the Trojan War. My daughter Ruth, the linguist, feels the last part is unduly restrictive. She says surely the word is the Greek *heros*, which meant 'protector' or 'defender', from the same Proto-Indo-European root as the Latin verb *servare*, which meant 'to safeguard'.

What exactly were Homer's heroes protecting, defending and safeguarding? Certainly not later conventions about good behaviour. Achilles – the star of the *Iliad* – was a psychopath given to red-mist homicidal rages. Not really the notion of the Greek state itself, either. The Trojan prince Hector, Troy's most formidable fighter – in other words the enemy – is the co-star of the *Iliad*, in which Homer calls him brave, bold, noble, courtly, peace-loving, thoughtful, a good son, husband and father, and entirely without a dark side to his nature. No partisan bias at all. At worst, in terms of manipulation, we're invited to see a murderous conflict between nation states as a necessary and noble thing. *Dulce et decorum est pro patria mori*, to quote twice from the future.

The *Odyssey* is the sequel to the *Iliad*, about – short version – a fighter named Odysseus, who spent ten years at the war, and then ten more getting home again afterward. Along the way he suffered many tests and trials. The stakes were high, because his wife Penelope was home alone, with their son Telemachus, and a rowdy crowd of suitors up to no good at all. More than anyone Odysseus codified the long-term, mainstream understanding of 'hero' —one who suffers, one who endures, one who survives a long and complicated journey through dangers and perils, and thereafter emerges with his honour and identity intact. Certainly that was how the word was instinctively understood by scholars in the nineteenth century. Any other educated person would have concurred, perhaps with a little confusion around the background verbs *protect*, *defend* and *safeguard*, which would have chimed in with late nineteenth-century norms about *noblesse oblige* and a sense of the common good. In fact Odysseus was motivated solely by personal pride, hubris and arrogance, but the nineteenth century preferred to imagine an element of altruism in his struggles. Thus by, say, the late 1880s (when the first use of *odyssey* as a common noun was recorded, meaning a long wandering or voyage marked by many changes of fortune) 'hero' meant, in practice, one who suffers, and endures, and survives a long and complicated journey through dangers and perils, in order to do good in some vague and unspecified way.

Felix Hoffmann was at the University of Munich in the late 1880s. The German chemist, who tried to synthesize codeine and ended up inventing something else entirely. He graduated magna cum laude, and then again two years later, with a doctorate, also magna cum laude. An educated man, no question. What was heroic about his invention? There are two possibilities, I think, in a nineteenth-century context. Either he wanted to imply his product had been on a long and complicated journey through dangers and perils, but it had survived, and it had emerged to do good, in the form of bringing pain relief and pleasure to the masses. Or possibly he wanted to imply his own personal work on the project had been a long and complicated journey through dangers and perils. Either version would have been absurd, given the accidental nature of the discovery. But vanity knows no bounds.

M y grandma was born two years after Hoffmann's product went on sale in Britain. (Maybe she was quietened down at night with his cough syrup.) She had 399,998 women standing behind her, and only one more to come ahead. The word 'hero' – and a lot of other words – were about to set out on long and complicated journeys of their own, through dangers and perils of their own. It was the age of the high-speed printing press, and mass-circulation newspapers, and monthlies, and scandal sheets, and popular mass-market fiction. By that point one whole generation had been through compulsory education, and a second was currently in school. Never before in history had more words been consumed more often by more people, or with more passion.

The word 'hero' itself fragmented into three separate things. A third of it stayed where it was, in the oak-panelled rooms of Oxford and Cambridge, with its classical definition endlessly refined and debated; a third of it was claimed by the establishment and its mouth-pieces for political use; and the final third came to mean nothing more than 'the main character in a popular book'. Each definition was in permanent uneasy conflict with the other two, especially the establishment's and the popular. At this point, five thousand years after the first proto-governments, the split between official heroes and folk heroes became definitive.

The split had been brewing for many centuries. The people of Britain (and Europe generally) had been governed for a long, long time, occasionally by remote and irrelevant rulers, but more often by intrusive and demanding tyrants, in a manner we find hard to imagine, accustomed as we are to democracy and the rule of law. Another of the books in our undergraduate bedroom was *Shakespeare Our*

Contemporary by Jan Kott. Kott was a Polish academic with a lifetime's experience of communist rule. He felt such a background was necessary to understand the paranoid political subtext in much of Shakespeare. He felt Elizabethan England was a vicious and capricious police state, not much better than Stalinist Russia. He was probably right. And Henry VIII was just as bad. And long before him we had the regency of Prince John, while Richard was away at the Crusades, during which time John ran the country like the head of a crime family. Which was when Robin Hood was invented.

Except not exactly. Robin Hood was first borrowed, then adapted, then established, then reinvented over and over again for hundreds of years. People continually looked back from a later perspective, and they thought, well, surely such a man really should have done this or that too, and those new details were added to the legend. As a whole it was a seamless and perfect example of everything we had ever learned about building a story, from the Stone Age onward.

What is the purpose of fiction? I think it can be summed up in a simple phrase: To give people what they don't get in real life. Originally it was courage and a sense of security; now it's a whole host of things. I used to live on a block that also housed a model agency. Every time I got on the subway, I found myself sitting opposite a supernaturally stunning nineteen-year-old. Of course in the real world I never spoke to her. I didn't ask her out to dinner. We didn't fly down to the islands for a steamy weekend. But we could in a book. Romance and romantic suspense is full of that stuff. In my own line of work – crime thrillers – I'm aware that readers need an antidote to an unsatisfactory everyday reality. If their car is stolen, they'll never get it back. If their house is burgled, they'll never see their stuff again, and the police will never catch the burglars. But they will in a book. Instead of a constant real-world buzz of low-level frustration, there will be a beginning, a middle and an end, by which time order will have been restored. A parallel or theoretical universe, where things happen, based on experience, but not constrained by fact, and from where the sheer satisfaction of a happy ending will osmose back into the real universe, in the form of contentment, compensation and consolation.

Thus peasants suffering Prince John's repressive taxation and brutal punishments no doubt idly dreamed of some tough, sparky guy who would show up and fix things for them. No doubt storytellers and balladeers immediately rushed to fill that need. Like working pros everywhere, they pulled what they had off the shelf and adapted it. They borrowed the name and the basic shape of the character from previous *chansons*, and then set about giving their listeners what they wanted. No doubt they started with those Stone Age principles: a suspenseful story full of dangers and perils, over which a memorable character would eventually triumph in a decisive manner, such that the listener finished with a tight and determined smile, and moist eyes fixed on the horizon. No doubt they improvised as they went along, in real time, sensing the listeners' mood, adding and subtracting as necessary. They gave Robin a superpower – archery – and narrowed the antagonist to a specific local flunky (the Sheriff of Nottingham), for enhanced focus and local resonance, and perhaps also for safety, because it was always better to disparage someone slightly lower down the hierarchy than the king.

Originally, Robin Hood was a regular guy. He was described in the earliest poems as a yeoman, which was a word with drifting meanings, bouncing up and down between a skilled agricultural labourer – like a miller – to a small freeholder. But in every definition a yeoman was a commoner, of no formal rank at all. Robin's sympathy for the downtrodden was clear from the start, as was his impatience with priests and clerics, his respect for women, and his opposition to the Sheriff of Nottingham. Some of his merry men were there in prototype form – Little John (an early proto-sidekick),

Much the miller's son, and Will Scarlet (although originally his name was less generic – usually Scarlock or Scathelock). Originally Robin had no views at all about Prince John's misrule or King Richard's splendour – in the earliest versions the monarchy is not mentioned at all (local opposition against Nottingham being enough for the narrative) and in one version the reigning king is given as Edward, not Richard.

Then came hundreds of years of edits, and cumulatively they are a perfect example of the push-pull pressures on a story, as various interested parties put their various oars in. The appeal of the tale was overwhelming and undeniable, so the establishment couldn't simply suppress it. Instead, like working pros everywhere, they adapted it. They fixed it in time during John's regency, at a historical distance which they felt was safe enough. It didn't exactly damage the notion of monarchy itself – in fact maybe it strengthened it, given the subliminal message that the actual monarch's absence had caused all the problems. Then came a call from the audience for more characters. Now we get this request on the phone from editors and producers: Can there be a love interest? Back then, the storytellers must have sensed restlessness in their listeners. So Maid Marian was brought on board. Then like storytellers everywhere, they realized they needed a comic figure. Friar Tuck was invented. And so on.

The establishment changed Robin himself most of all. First they made him a strong supporter of King Richard (see above – preserve the monarchy by throwing John under the bus) and then they started to inch him up the social scale, in what seems to have been a permanent and irresistible pressure on any British narrative, true or imagined. I suppose it was a class thing. Like Shakespeare – obviously such a genius can't just have been an oik from the Midlands, so clearly he was really the Earl of Oxford. In Robin's case, such a sturdy and beloved Englishman can't have been just a yeoman. So by the end of the sixteenth century he was the Earl of Huntingdon. The audience went along with the conceit, and the fundamental description of a folk hero was cemented in place – a person of status, in some way cast out, breaking the rules for a just purpose.

This basic specification had been foreshadowed before, and would be repeated again. For instance, I remember reading Ovid's retelling of the Theseus legend, in school, in Latin. On the bus home I was reading *Dr. No* by Ian Fleming. And I noticed I was reading the same story, two thousand years later. A man of rank (a prince; a Commander in the Royal Navy) not exactly cast out but disapproved of and barely tolerated, fights a grotesque opponent in a secret underground lair, with the help of a woman from the other side (Ariadne; Honey Ryder) and technological intervention (the ball of twine; Q's arsenal) and comes home to a mixed reception. The form was durable.

I used it myself, unconsciously, when I started writing. I needed a main character, but felt that overthinking his specification would beat the life out of him, so I wrote based on instinct – which is to say, based on everything I had ever read and subliminally absorbed before. And sure enough, Jack Reacher turned out to be a man of rank (a major, a West Point graduate) now cast out from mainstream society (albeit voluntarily, by his own hand) and dispensing rough justice outside the mainstream rules. (Very rough justice – I saw a capsule description of the Reacher series on the internet that said, 'This is a detective series in which the detective commits more homicides than he solves'.) As such, Reacher slotted very neatly into the folk hero tradition, specifically the knight errant subgroup, which seems to be universal in appeal – as in, for instance, the Japanese *ronin* myths, in which a samurai, disowned by his master, is sentenced to wander the land, doing good. For me the trope was so strong it overrode common sense and quotidian realism, in that the hands-on experiences implied in Reacher's backstory are those of an

NCO or warrant officer, not those of a commissioned officer, and almost certainly not those of a West Point graduate. But my subconscious led me to the knight errant myth, and a knight errant must have been a knight to start with, so a major he was. Military insiders are very aware of the discrepancy, but they still enjoy the fiction – which I take as proof of the power of that ancient, evolved story structure.

The political use of the word 'hero' started with the dawn of mass communication and continues today. First its definition became detached from classical notions of protracted journeys and struggles, and it became a word bestowed upon anyone who did any brave and good thing – an honour always in the gift of the establishment or its mouthpieces. The downward direction of the dispensation, in terms of social class, is best observed in old newsreels of, say, the FA Cup Final. First the fruity voice on the crackly soundtrack patronizes the spectators (usually northerners, 'up' in London 'for the cup') and then there's some game action, and a sentence of commentary, dripping with irony, saying something like, 'The hero of the hour was

Stanley Matthews'. Dripping with irony, in order to emphasize the purely metaphorical use of the word, as if to say, obviously a common footballer can't really be a hero, but we'll say so anyway, to indicate how caught up we are in the cloth-cap-wearing ferret-lovers' passion. (Although Matthews was knighted later, thereby perhaps becoming capable of unironic heroism.)

More sinister was a migration away from mere description (be it ironic, halfhearted or wholehearted) toward the pre-emption or influence of debate. The 1919 Housing Act – which proposed significant public expenditures – was boosted by the slogan 'Homes Fit For Heroes'. It's hard to say out loud (because of a century of pre-emption and influence) but of course most First World War soldiers were not heroes by any definition – many served in a reluctant and desultory manner. Army slang is full of terms for malingerers. No doubt their experiences were horribly unpleasant and uncomfortable, but the automatic association of 'soldier' with 'hero' was explicitly political, as it still is, and served to short-circuit discussion, as it still does. The establishment press responds to, say, a controversy about an individual soldier's actions long ago during the Irish Troubles, by mounting a campaign that could be headlined 'Hands Off Our Heroes'. The nudging 'heroes' is compounded by the 'our' – a smug, wheedling assumption of agreement, intended to prompt, even coerce, and equally to suggest the presence of an 'other' who doesn't share 'our' values. A toxic atmosphere can quickly be created, both physically – in 1918, in Phoenix, Arizona, a man declined to buy a Victory Bond (he couldn't afford one) and was beaten to death by the crowd – and mentally, in that criticism of military actions and behaviours is now effectively forbidden, especially in America. Instead, we are invited to 'Salute Our Heroes', and let them board the airplane first, even though the beneficiary of our coerced cooperation is probably a warehouse clerk deployed to New Jersey.

Bestowal from-on-high of the plaudit inevitably became ridiculous. A school-crossing keeper is called a 'hero' for working for forty years. The England football team survive a group stage in an international tournament and the players are called 'heroes'. Combining both the trivial and the coercive, I just got a flyer from the Department of Motor Vehicles in Wyoming, where I live part-time. It is headlined 'Anyone Can Be a Hero'. It says that if you have the donor symbol on your driver's licence (I do) then you have made 'the heroic decision to save and heal lives by donating your organs, eyes and tissues at the time of your death'. So now having your corpse cut up when you're already dead is enough to guarantee heroic status.

For these reasons and more I avoid the word, and distrust the concept. I have no heroes and recognize none. 'The main character in a popular book' is good enough for me, especially if that character lights up the circuits that evolution has wired inside me. I need encouraging, empowering, emboldening and consoling, the same as anyone else. Happily there are a lot of writers who know that. They aren't dumb. I have needs, they have aims. Together we purr along, in a system designed by the ages. All good.

Except not really. There's a problem with my 1,198-times great grandmother. There's an unthinking assumption that evolution is always progress, natural and inevitable. Like farming. Scientists don't always question this assumption. They can't. Just the facts, ma'am, and what they can prove, and so on. They can explain the science in amazing detail, and they can show you astonishing DNA research, and they can say with confidence that perhaps as few as two thousand breeding pairs of humans survived the last glaciation on the whole of the landmass we now call Europe. But their necessary anodyne academic-journal tone slides on by too quickly. They say, 'Four thousand lucky people survived'. The novelist stops and thinks, OK, but who were those people?

Conventionally our long, eventful seven-million-year evolutionary journey is thought of as an inevitable ascent toward ever-increasing perfection. Which it might be. Or not. It depends on where we started. Who are we descended from? Who was my 1,198-times great grandmother? What kind of person survives an eight-hundred-generation Ice Age? Such a thing doesn't happen by accident. Potential survivors didn't sit around hoping for the best. They spent eight hundred generations kicking and clawing and killing and stealing. Maybe they started on the Neanderthals. Then they started on each other. Conditions got worse. The nice guys died out. By the end the human population was reduced to the nastiest handful. My 1,198-times great grandmother was one of them. One of a savage, feral, cunning bunch. They would kill you as soon as look at you. They would steal your food and shelter. A ferocious will to live, with the emphasis on the first part. My ancestors. Hopefully diluted by subsequent random mutations, but to at least some degree, and always, a part of me, and of the characters I like to read, and the characters I like to write.

TLS

Enjoyed the book?

Subscribe to the *TLS* today at just £1/$1 a week for 6 weeks.

As a *TLS* subscriber, you'll enjoy:

- The weekly *TLS* print edition, delivered straight to your door
- Full access to the *TLS* app on smartphone and tablet
- Unrestricted access to the-tls.co.uk and the *TLS* archive (going back to 1902)
- The weekly *TLS* e-newsletter
- Every *TLS* podcast

Save up to 60% today.

Go to the-tls.co.uk/LCSUB to subscribe.

Dollar currency is USD. Saving based on comparison against *TLS* Complete Works full UK subscription price. Correct at August 2019. Visit the-tls.co.uk/terms for full T&Cs.

Also from TLS Books

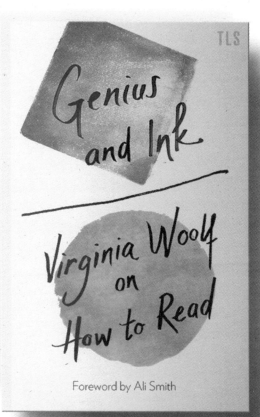

Who better to serve as a guide to great
books and their authors than
Virginia Woolf?